A
FAILURE
TO
NETWORK

SARAH MARRIE BURGE

ISBN: **1466479639**
ISBN-13: **978-1466479630**

DEDICATION

To Crystal Jo Etheridge, My over Zealous Socialite.

Warning: This book is a list of social networks to help parents, who love their children block them so that they cannot get harmed mentally by the idiots out there who get off on hurting little ones and big ones.

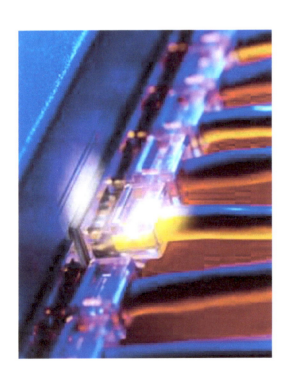

CONTENTS

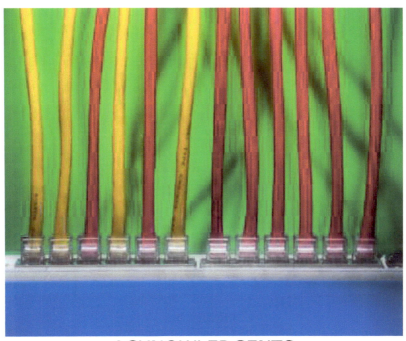

ACKNOWLEDGENTS

Thank you Wikipedia and the www.

CHAPTER 1 - LIST OF SOCIAL NETWORKING WEBSITES

THIS IS A LIST OF MAJOR ACTIVE SOCIAL NETWORKING WEBSITES AND EXCLUDES DATING WEBSITES (SEE LIST OF ONLINE DATING WEBSITES). FOR DEFUNCT SOCIAL NETWORKING WEBSITES, SEE LIST OF DEFUNCT SOCIAL NETWORKING WEBSITES. PLEASE NOTE THE LIST IS NOT EXHAUSTIVE, AND IS LIMITED TO NOTABLE, WELL-KNOWN SITES.
NAME
DESCRIPTION/FOCUS
DATE LAUNCHED REGISTERED USERS
REGISTRATION   GLOBAL ALEXA1 PAGE RANKING

ACADEMIA.EDU
SOCIAL NETWORKING SITE FOR ACADEMICS/RESEARCHERS   SEPTEMBER 2008
2110002

OPEN 60533

ADVOGATO
FREE AND OPEN SOURCE SOFTWARE DEVELOPERS
1999 135754
OPEN 1445995 [[FRIENDWARPED.WALL.FM
HTTP://FRIENDWARPED.WALL.FM/

ANOBII
BOOKS 2006 OPEN 119326

ASMALLWORLD
EUROPEAN JET SET AND SOCIAL ELITE WORLD-WIDE
MARCH 2004 5500007
INVITE-ONLY
61928

ASIANAVENUE
A SOCIAL NETWORK FOR THE ASIAN AMERICAN
COMMUNITY 1997 OPEN 758549

ATHLINKS
RUNNING, SWIMMING 2001 13945810
OPEN 3712911

AUDIMATED.COM
INDEPENDENT MUSIC 2010 OPEN 74785712

BADOO
GENERAL, MEET NEW PEOPLE, POPULAR IN EUROPE
AND LATIN AMERICA 2006 8600000013
OPEN TO PEOPLE 18 AND OLDER 11714

BEBO
GENERAL JULY 2005 11700000015
OPEN TO PEOPLE 13 AND OLDER 227916

BIGADDA

INDIAN SOCIAL NETWORKING SITE   AUGUST 2007
300000017
OPEN TO PEOPLE 16 AND OLDER   1290318

BIIP.NO

NORWEGIAN COMMUNITY   JUNE 1, 2005 43000019
REQUIRES NORWEGIAN PHONE NUMBER   4246820

BLACKPLANET

AFRICAN-AMERICANS   SEPTEMBER 1, 1999
2000000021
OPEN   586322

BLAUK

ANYONE WHO WANTS TO TELL SOMETHING ABOUT A
STRANGER OR ACQUAINTANCE.   2010   OPEN
TO PEOPLE 13 AND OLDER. 46379623

BLOGSTER

BLOGGING COMMUNITY NOVEMBER 24, 2005
8557924
OPEN   1014425

BOLT.COM

GENERAL   1996   OPEN   11106926

BUSUU

LANGUAGE LEARNING COMMUNITY   MAY 16, 2008
400000027
OPEN   433028

BUZZNET

MUSIC AND POP-CULTURE   2005   1000000029
OPEN   122730

CAFEMOM

MOTHERS DECEMBER 2006 125000031
OPEN TO MOMS AND MOMS-TO-BE   149232

CAKE FINANCIAL
INVESTING   SEPTEMBER 17, 2007   OPEN
48192233

CARE2
GREEN LIVING AND SOCIAL ACTIVISM   1998
996194734
OPEN   188335

CARINGBRIDGE
NOT FOR PROFIT PROVIDING FREE WEBSITES THAT
CONNECT FAMILY AND FRIENDS DURING A SERIOUS
HEALTH EVENT, CARE AND RECOVERY.36
950000037
OPEN TO PEOPLE 18 AND OLDER38
39

CELLUFUN
MOBILE SOCIAL GAME NETWORK, NUMBER 8 US
MOBILE WEBSITE40
2007   300000041
OPEN TO PEOPLE 14 AND OLDER   11551142

CLASSMATES.COM
SCHOOL, COLLEGE, WORK AND THE MILITARY
1995   5000000043
OPEN TO PEOPLE 18 AND OLDER44
296145

CLOOB
GENERAL. POPULAR IN IRAN   2004   OPEN
91446

COUCHSURFING

WORLDWIDE NETWORK FOR MAKING CONNECTIONS BETWEEN TRAVELERS AND THE LOCAL COMMUNITIES THEY VISIT.   2003   296742147
OPEN   182148

COZYCOT
EAST ASIAN AND SOUTHEAST ASIAN WOMEN
2001   15000049
OPEN   371150

CROSS.TV
FAITH BASED SOCIAL NETWORK FOR CHRISTIAN BELIEVERS FROM AROUND THE WORLD   2008
45000051
OPEN   3171652

CRUNCHYROLL
ANIME AND FORUMS.   2006   OPEN   515353

CYWORLD
GENERAL. POPULAR IN SOUTH KOREA.   1999
2400000054
OPEN   102055

DAILYBOOTH
PHOTO-BLOGGING SITE WHERE USERS UPLOAD A PHOTO EVERY DAY   FEBRUARY 13, 2009   OPEN   501456

DAILYSTRENGTH
MEDICAL & EMOTIONAL SUPPORT COMMUNITY - PHYSICAL HEALTH, MENTAL HEALTH, SUPPORT GROUPS   NOVEMBER 4, 2007   OPEN   2205457

DECAYENNE
EUROPEAN AND AMERICAN SOCIAL ELITE 2001
INVITE-ONLY

126394358

DELICIOUS

SOCIAL BOOKMARKING ALLOWING USERS TO LOCATE AND SAVE WEBSITES THAT MATCH THEIR OWN INTERESTS   SEPTEMBER 2003882292159
OPEN 27260

DEVIANTART

ART COMMUNITY   AUGUST 7, 2000 904096261
OPEN 12662

DIASPORA*

DECENTRALIZED, PRIVACY AWARE, GENERAL (OPEN SOURCE) NOVEMBER, 2010   OPEN 249476364

DISABOOM

PEOPLE WITH DISABILITIES (AMPUTEE, CEREBRAL PALSY, MS, AND OTHER DISABILITIES)
OPEN 27569865

DOL2DAY

POLITIC COMMUNITY, SOCIAL NETWORK, INTERNET RADIO (GERMAN-SPEAKING COUNTRIES)
4020066
OPEN 88704767

DONTSTAYIN

CLUBBING (PRIMARILY UK)   OPEN 5409568

DRAUGIEM.LV

GENERAL (PRIMARILY LV, LT, HU)   260046669
INVITATION ONLY   291570

DOUBAN

CHINESE WEB 2.0 WEBSITE PROVIDING USER REVIEW AND RECOMMENDATION SERVICES FOR MOVIES, BOOKS, AND MUSIC. 2005   4685000071
OPEN 11972

DXY.CN
CHINESE ONLINE COMMUNITY FOR PHYSICIANS, HEALTH CARE PROFESSIONALS, PHARMACIES AND FACILITIES   200073
200000074
OPEN 1400575

ELFTOWN
COMMUNITY AND WIKI AROUND FANTASY AND SCI-FI.
18500076
OPEN, APPROVAL NEEDED   4327777

ELIXIO
HIGH-NET-WORTH INDIVIDUALS, YOUNG BUSINESS EXECUTIVES JULY 2007 40000 78
INVITE-ONLY 15364679

EPERNICUS
FOR RESEARCH SCIENTISTS
OPEN 52808380

EONS.COM
FOR BABY BOOMERS
OPEN TO PEOPLE 13 AND OLDER   3424081

EXPERIENCE PROJECT
LIFE EXPERIENCES   OPEN 345282

EXPLOROO

TRAVEL SOCIAL NETWORKING.   OPEN
20986883

FACEBOOK
GENERAL.   FEBRUARY 2004 640000000+84
OPEN TO PEOPLE 13 AND OLDER   285

FACEPARTY
GENERAL. POPULAR UK.   20000086
INVITATION ONLY TO PEOPLE 18 AND OLDER
2876087

FACES.COM
ADULT SOCIAL NETWORK, MAINLY UK & USA 2011
70000088
OPEN TO PEOPLE 18 AND OLDER WORLDWIDE
15969389

FETLIFE
PEOPLE WHO ARE INTO BDSM   50000090
OPEN TO PEOPLE "OF [LEGAL] AGE TO SEE ADULT
CONTENT"   551391

FILMAFFINITY
MOVIES AND TV SERIES   2002   25000092
OPEN   391693

FLEDGEWING
ENTREPRENEURAL COMMUNITY TARGETED TOWARDS
WORLDWIDE UNIVERSITY STUDENTS   OPEN
TO UNIVERSITY STUDENTS 179399094

FLIXSTER
MOVIES   2007 6300000095
OPEN TO PEOPLE 13 AND OLDER   101896

FLICKR

PHOTO SHARING, COMMENTING, PHOTOGRAPHY RELATED NETWORKING, WORLDWIDE FEBRUARY 2004   3200000097
OPEN TO PEOPLE 13 AND OLDER (YAHOO! LOGIN) 3198

FOCUS.COM
BUSINESS TO BUSINESS, WORLDWIDE   2005
85000099
OPEN TO PEOPLE 13 AND OLDER   11495100

FOTKI
PHOTO SHARING, VIDEO HOSTING, PHOTO CONTESTS, JOURNALS, FORUMS, FLEXIBLE PRIVACY PROTECTION, FRIEND'S FEED, AUDIO COMMENTS AND UNLIMITED CUSTOM DESIGN INTEGRATION. OCTOBER 1998   1632565   OPEN   5367101

FOTOLOG
PHOTOBLOGGING. POPULAR IN SOUTH AMERICA AND SPAIN   20000000102
OPEN   1194103

FOURSQUARE
LOCATION BASED MOBILE SOCIAL NETWORK
10000000104
OPEN   625105

FRIENDS REUNITED
UK BASED. SCHOOL, COLLEGE, WORK, SPORT AND STREETS   19000000106
OPEN TO PEOPLE 13 AND OLDER   10231107

FRIENDSTER
GENERAL. POPULAR IN SOUTHEAST ASIA. NO LONGER POPULAR IN THE WESTERN WORLD
2002   90000000108

OPEN TO PEOPLE 16 AND OLDER.   979109

FRÜHSTÜCKSTREFF
GENERAL JULY 2001 14800 OPEN   1253155110

FUBAR
DATING, AN "ONLINE BAR" FOR 18 AND OLDER
OCTOBER 2007   1200000111
OPEN TO PEOPLE 18+   9476112

GAIA ONLINE
ANIME AND GAMES. POPULAR IN USA, CANADA AND
EUROPE. MODERATELY POPULAR AROUND ASIA.
23523663113
OPEN TO PEOPLE 13 AND OLDER   1071114

GAMERDNA
COMPUTER AND VIDEO GAMES SEPTEMBER 21, 2006
310000115
OPEN   22887116

GATHER.COM
ARTICLE, PICTURE, AND VIDEO SHARING, AS WELL
AS GROUP DISCUSSIONS   465000117
OPEN   3974118

GAYS.COM
SOCIAL NETWORK FOR LGBT COMMUNITY, GUIDE
FOR LGBT BARS, RESTAURANTS, CLUBS, SHOPPING
MAY 16, 2008 100000119
OPEN, GLOBAL   74664120

GENI.COM
FAMILIES, GENEALOGY JANUARY 16, 2007
15000000121
OPEN   5815122

GOGOYOKO
FAIR PLAY IN MUSIC - SOCIAL NETWORKING SITE FOR MUSICIANS AND MUSIC LOVERS   INVITE ONLY WHILE IN BETA   119272123

GOODREADS
LIBRARY CATALOGING, BOOK LOVERS   DECEMBER 2006   OPEN   2543124

GOODWIZZ
SOCIAL NETWORK WITH MATCHMAKING AND PERSONALITY GAMES TO FIND NEW CONTACTS. GLOBAL, BASED IN FRANCE.   OCTOBER 2010   110000125126
OPEN   214214127

GOOGLE+
GENERAL JUNE 28, 2011   50000000128
GENERAL, OPEN NA (ALEXA ONLY RECORDS DATA FOR SECOND-LEVEL DOMAINS)

GOOGLE BUZZ
GENERAL FEBRUARY 9, 2010129
OPEN   NA (ALEXA ONLY RECORDS DATA FOR SECOND-LEVEL DOMAINS)

GOVLOOP
FOR PEOPLE IN AND AROUND GOVERNMENT   91852130

GRONO.NET
POLAND
2000000   OPEN   2958131

HABBO
GENERAL FOR TEENS. OVER 31 COMMUNITIES WORLDWIDE. CHAT ROOM AND USER PROFILES.

200000000132133134
OPEN TO PEOPLE 13 AND OLDER   6545135

HI5
GENERAL. POPULAR IN INDIA, MONGOLIA, THAILAND, ROMANIA, JAMAICA, CENTRAL AFRICA, PORTUGAL AND LATIN AMERICA. NOT VERY POPULAR IN THE USA.
2003   80000000136
OPEN TO PEOPLE 13 AND OLDER.   443137

HOSPITALITY CLUB
HOSPITALITY   328629138
OPEN   38258139

HOTLIST
GEO-SOCIAL AGGREGATOR ROOTED IN THE CONCEPT OF KNOWING WHERE YOUR FRIENDS ARE, WERE, AND WILL BE.   80000140
OPEN   28241141

HR.COM
SOCIAL NETWORKING SITE FOR HUMAN RESOURCES PROFESSIONALS 1999   194000142
OPEN   60048143

HUB CULTURE
GLOBAL INFLUENCERS FOCUSED ON WORTH CREATION   NOVEMBER 2002 20000144
INVITE-ONLY
515308145

HYVES
GENERAL, MOSTLY POPULAR IN THE NETHERLANDS.
SEPTEMBER 200410097000146
OPEN   658147

IBIBO
TALENT BASED SOCIAL NETWORKING SITE THAT
ALLOWS TO PROMOTE ONE'S SELF AND ALSO
DISCOVER NEW TALENT. MOST POPULAR IN INDIA.
3500000148
OPEN   695149

IDENTI.CA
TWITTER-LIKE SERVICE POPULAR WITH HACKERS
AND SOFTWARE FREEDOM ADVOCATES.   395695
OPEN   3822150

INDABA MUSIC
ONLINE COLLABORATION FOR MUSICIANS, REMIX
CONTESTS, AND NETWORKING.   350000151
OPEN, GLOBAL   55062152

IRC-GALLERIA
FINLAND   505000153
OPEN TO FINNISH SPEAKING PEOPLE 12 AND OLDER
3302154

ITALKI.COM
LANGUAGE LEARNING SOCIAL NETWORK. 100+
LANGUAGES.   500000155
OPEN, GLOBAL   29939156

INTERNATIONS
INTERNATIONAL COMMUNITY   INVITE-ONLY
25604157

ITSMY
MOBILE COMMUNITY WORLDWIDE, BLOGGING,
FRIENDS, PERSONAL TV-SHOWS   2500000158
206437159

IWIW

HUNGARY
4000000160
INVITE-ONLY
532161

JAIKU
GENERAL. MICROBLOGGING. OWNED BY GOOGLE
FEBRUARY 2006   OPEN TO PEOPLE 13 AND OLDER
15661162

KAIXIN001
GENERAL. IN SIMPLIFIED CHINESE; CATERS FOR
MAINLAND CHINA USERS   OPEN TO THE
GENERAL PUBLIC   183163

KIWIBOX
GENERAL.   1999   2400000164
OPEN TO PEOPLE 13 AND OLDER   104563165

LAFANGO
TALENT-FOCUSED MEDIA SHARING SITE
OPEN, GLOBAL   151301166

LAIBHAARI
MARATHI SOCIAL NETWORKING   2010   100000
OPEN   29,782167

LAST.FM
MUSIC   2002   30000000168
OPEN   552169

LIBRARYTHING
BOOK LOVERS   AUGUST 29, 2005   1300000170
OPEN TO PEOPLE 13 AND OLDER   8243171

LIFEKNOT

SHARED INTERESTS, HOBBIES   OPEN TO PEOPLE 18 AND OLDER 602117172

LINKEDIN
BUSINESS AND PROFESSIONAL NETWORKING   MAY 2003   120000000173
OPEN TO PEOPLE 18 AND OLDER   13174

LINKEXPATS
SOCIAL NETWORKING WEBSITE FOR EXPATRIATES. 100+ COUNTRIES.   OPEN, GLOBAL 1668484175

LISTOGRAPHY
LISTS. AUTOBIOGRAPHY   OPEN 197009176

LIVEJOURNAL
BLOGGING. POPULAR IN RUSSIA AND AMONG THE RUSSIAN-SPEAKING DIASPORA ABROAD. APRIL 15, 1999   17564977177
OPEN (OPENID)
76178

LIVEMOCHA
ONLINE LANGUAGE LEARNING   5000000179
OPEN 4079180

LUNARSTORM
SWEDEN   1200000181
OPEN 65874182

MAKEOUTCLUB
GENERAL AUGUST 9, 1999   OPEN 723381183

MEETIN
GENERAL   OPEN 173717184

MEETUP.COM
GENERAL. USED TO PLAN OFFLINE MEETINGS FOR PEOPLE INTERESTED IN VARIOUS ACTIVITIES
OPEN TO PEOPLE 18 AND OLDER   739185

MEETTHEBOSS
BUSINESS AND FINANCE COMMUNITY, WORLDWIDE.
OPEN   107180186

MIXI
JAPAN
OCTOBER 25, 2000   24323160187
INVITE-ONLY
140188

MOBIKADE
MOBILE COMMUNITY, UK ONLY   OPEN TO PEOPLE 18 AND OLDER   1851728189

MOCOSPACE
MOBILE COMMUNITY, WORLDWIDE
3000000190
OPEN TO PEOPLE 14 AND OLDER   3685191

MOG
MUSIC   OPEN TO PEOPLE 14 AND OLDER
4221192

MOUTHSHUT.COM
SOCIAL NETWORK, SOCIAL MEDIA, CONSUMER REVIEWS   OPEN   2545193

MUBI (WEBSITE)
AUTEUR CINEMA   200000   OPEN   25648194

MULTIPLY

"REAL WORLD" RELATIONSHIPS. POPULAR IN
PRIMARILY IN ASIA.
10000000195
OPEN TO PEOPLE 13 AND OLDER. 382196

MUXLIM
MUSLIM PORTAL SITE   2006 50000197
OPEN TO PEOPLE 13 AND OLDER   59099198

MYANIMELIST
ANIME THEMED SOCIAL COMMUNITY   160000199
OPEN TO PEOPLE 13 AND OLDER   6096200

MYHERITAGE
FAMILY-ORIENTED SOCIAL NETWORK SERVICE
30000000 201
OPEN 2953202

MYLIFE
LOCATING FRIENDS AND FAMILY, KEEPING IN TOUCH
(FORMERLY REUNION.COM)
51000000203
OPEN 1481204

MY OPERA
BLOGGING, MOBILE BLOGGING, PHOTO SHARING,
CONNECTING WITH FRIENDS, OPERA LINK AND
OPERA UNITE. GLOBAL   7300000205
OPEN NA (ALEXA ONLY RECORDS DATA FOR
SECOND-LEVEL DOMAINS)

MYSPACE
GENERAL AUGUST 2003100000000+206207
OPEN TO AGES 13 AND OLDER.   86208

MYYEARBOOK
GENERAL, CHARITY   20000000209

OPEN TO AGE 13 AND UP & GRADES 9 AND UP
851210

NASZA-KLASA.PL
SCHOOL, COLLEGE AND FRIENDS. POPULAR IN
POLAND   11000000211
OPEN 40961212

NETLOG
GENERAL. POPULAR IN EUROPE, TURKEY, THE ARAB
WORLD AND CANADA'S QUÉBEC PROVINCE.
FORMERLY KNOWN AS FACEBOX AND REDBOX.213
70000000214
OPEN TO PEOPLE 13 AND OLDER   296215

NETTBY
NORWEGIAN COMMUNITY   SEPTEMBER 14, 2006
OPEN 2719216

NEXOPIA
CANADA   1400000217
OPEN TO PEOPLE 13 AND OLDER 218
24071219

NGO POST
NON-PROFIT NEWS SHARING AND NETWORKING,
MAINLY IN INDIA   15000220
OPEN 70134221

NING
USERS CREATE THEIR OWN SOCIAL WEBSITES AND
SOCIAL NETWORKS   OPEN TO PEOPLE 13 AND
OLDER   273222

ODNOKLASSNIKI

CONNECT WITH OLD CLASSMATES. POPULAR IN RUSSIA AND FORMER SOVIET REPUBLICS
45000000223
OPEN   104224

ONECLIMATE
NOT FOR PROFIT SOCIAL NETWORKING AND CLIMATE CHANGE
OPEN TO PEOPLE OF ALL AGES AND LOCATIONS   307773225

ONEWORLDTV
NOT FOR PROFIT VIDEO SHARING AND SOCIAL NETWORKING AIMED AT PEOPLE INTERESTED IN SOCIAL ISSUES, DEVELOPMENT, ENVIRONMENT, ETC.
OPEN   27434227226

OPEN DIARY
FIRST ONLINE BLOGGING COMMUNITY, FOUNDED IN 1998   1998   5000000227
OPEN TO PEOPLE 13 AND OLDER   39290228

ORKUT
GENERAL. OWNED BY GOOGLE INC. POPULAR IN INDIA AND BRAZIL.229
JANUARY 22, 2004   100000000230
OPEN TO PEOPLE 18 AND OLDER, (GOOGLE LOGIN) 106231

OUTEVERYWHERE
GAY/LGBTQ COMMUNITY   OPEN   329887232

PASSPORTSTAMP
TRAVEL   OPEN   366598233

PATIENTSLIKEME

ONLINE COMMUNITY FOR PATIENTS WITH LIFE-CHANGING ILLNESSES TO FIND OTHER PATIENTS LIKE THEM, SHARE THEIR DATA WITH OTHERS, AND LEARN MORE ABOUT THEIR CONDITION TO IMPROVE THEIR OUTCOME.   2006   109587234
OPEN TO PEOPLE 13 YEARS AND UP   57962235

PARTYFLOCK
DUTCH VIRTUAL COMMUNITY FOR PEOPLE INTERESTED IN HOUSE MUSIC AND OTHER ELECTRONIC DANCE MUSIC   NOVEMBER 10, 2001   321125   OPEN TO PEOPLE 18 YEARS AND UP   7226236

PINGSTA
COLLABORATIVE PLATFORM FOR THE WORLD'S INTERNETWORK EXPERTS
INVITE-ONLY, ONLY INTERNET EXPERTS
1668955237

PLAXO
AGGREGATOR   15000000238
OPEN   1533239

PLAYAHEAD
SWEDISH, DANISH TEENAGERS   CLOSED
63081240

PUREVOLUME
CONNECTING INDIE MUSIC BANDS AND LISTENERS, THROUGH MUSIC SHARING AND SOCIAL NETWORKING   2003   OPEN   20822241

PLAYFIRE
COMPUTER AND VIDEO GAMES   OPEN TO PEOPLE 13 AND OLDER 62555242

PLAYLIST.COM
GENERAL, MUSIC   OPEN TO PEOPLE OVER 13 4340243

PLURK
MICRO-BLOGGING, RSS, UPDATES. VERY POPULAR IN TAIWAN
OPEN   1072244

PRESENT.LY
ENTERPRISE SOCIAL NETWORKING AND MICRO-BLOGGING   OPEN 4893711245

QAPACITY
A A BUSINESS-ORIENTED SOCIAL NETWORKING SITE AND A BUSINESS DIRECTORY   OPEN TO PEOPLE 16 AND OLDER 96847246

QUECHUP
GENERAL, FRIENDSHIP, DATING   2007   OPEN TO THOSE OVER 16 150757247

QZONE
GENERAL. IN SIMPLIFIED CHINESE; CATERS FOR MAINLAND CHINA USERS   480000000248249
OPEN TO THE GENERAL PUBLIC   NA (ALEXA ONLY RECORDS DATA FOR SECOND-LEVEL DOMAINS)

RAPTR
VIDEO GAMES   OPEN 25664250

RAVELRY
KNITTING AND CROCHET   743930251
OPEN 7811252

RENREN

SIGNIFICANT SITE IN CHINA. WAS KNOWN AS 校内 (XIAONEI) UNTIL AUGUST 2009.   160000000253
OPEN 83254

RESEARCHGATE
SOCIAL NETWORK FOR SCIENTIFIC RESEARCHERS
400000255
OPEN 23095256

REVERBNATION.COM
SOCIAL NETWORK FOR MUSICIAN AND BANDS
500000257
OPEN TO PEOPLE 16 AND OLDER   4422258

RYZE
BUSINESS   500000259
OPEN 19839260

SCIENCESTAGE
SCIENCE-ORIENTED MULTIMEDIA PLATFORM AND NETWORK FOR SCIENTISTS   OPEN
26804261

SCISPACE.NET
COLLABORATIVE NETWORK SITE FOR SCIENTISTS BY INVITATION, BUT CAN REQUEST AN INVITATION 1231795262

SHARETHEMUSIC
MUSIC COMMUNITY. SHARING AND LISTENING TO MUSIC FOR FREE AND LEGALLY   OPEN
471712263

SHELFARI
BOOKS   OCTOBER 11, 2006   OPEN 19681264

SKYROCK
SOCIAL NETWORK IN FRENCH-SPEAKING WORLD
22000000265
OPEN   437266

SOCIAL_LIFE_(WEBSITE)
BRAZILIAN JET SET AND SOCIAL ELITE WORLD-WIDE
2008   550000267
INVITE-ONLY
154533268

SOCIALVIBE
SOCIAL NETWORK FOR CHARITY   435000
OPEN   41927269

SONICO.COM
GENERAL. POPULAR IN LATIN AMERICA AND SPANISH
AND PORTUGUESE SPEAKING REGIONS.
17000000270271
OPEN TO PEOPLE 13 AND OLDER   507272

SOUNDCLOUD
REPOSITORY OF ORIGINAL MUSIC PIECES AND
NETWORKING.   1000000273
OPEN   374274

STICKAM
LIVE VIDEO STREAMING AND CHAT.
2000000275
OPEN   2742276

STUDIVZ
UNIVERSITY STUDENTS, MOSTLY IN THE GERMAN-
SPEAKING COUNTRIES. SCHOOL STUDENTS AND
THOSE OUT OF EDUCATION SIGN UP VIA ITS
PARTNER SITES SCHÜLERVZ AND MEINVZ.
17000000277

OPEN   1318278

STUMBLEUPON
STUMBLE THROUGH WEBSITES THAT MATCH YOUR SELECTED INTERESTS   10600000279
OPEN   108280

TAGGED
GENERAL.   100000000281
OPEN   281282

TALENTTROVE
ONLINE TALENT NETWORK   OPEN   21177283

TALKBIZNOW
BUSINESS NETWORKING   OPEN   283770284

TALTOPIA
ONLINE ARTISTIC COMMUNITY   OPEN   52759285

TARINGA!
GENERAL   11000000286
OPEN TO PEOPLE 13 AND OLDER   137287

TEACHSTREET
EDUCATION / LEARNING / TEACHING - MORE THAN 400 SUBJECTS   OPEN   61492288

TERMWIKI
LEARNING / LANGUAGES / TRANSLATION - 1.2M TERMS IN MORE THAN 1300 SUBJECTS   MAY 2010
OPEN   16182289

TRAVBUDDY.COM
TRAVEL   2005   1588000290

OPEN TO PEOPLE 18 AND OLDER   11789291

TRAVELLERSPOINT
TRAVEL   2002   310000292
OPEN   11486293

TRIBE.NET
GENERAL   OPEN 5706294

TROMBI.COM
FRENCH SUBSIDIARY OF CLASSMATES.COM
4400000295
7283296

TUENTI
SPANISH-BASED UNIVERSITY AND HIGH SCHOOL
SOCIAL NETWORK. VERY POPULAR IN SPAIN
4500000   INVITE-ONLY 730297

TUMBLR
GENERAL. MICRO-BLOGGING, RSS 2007   OPEN
46298

TWITTER
GENERAL. MICRO-BLOGGING, RSS, UPDATES   JULY
15, 2006   175000000299300
OPEN 9301

VKONTAKTE
SOCIAL NETWORK FOR RUSSIAN-SPEAKING WORLD
INCLUDING FORMER SOVIET REPUBLICS. SEPTEMBER
2006   110578500302
OPEN 44303

VAMPIREFREAKS.COM
GOTHIC AND INDUSTRIAL SUBCULTURE   1999
1931049304

OPEN TO USERS 13 AND OVER 7577305

VIADEO
GLOBAL SOCIAL NETWORKING AND CAMPUS NETWORKING AVAILABLE IN ENGLISH, FRENCH, GERMAN, SPANISH, ITALIAN AND PORTUGUESE 35000000306
OPEN 710307

VIRB
SOCIAL NETWORK THAT FOCUSES HEAVILY ON ARTISTS, INCLUDING MUSICIANS AND PHOTOGRAPHERS   2007   OPEN 22474308

VOX
BLOGGING   OPEN 1319309

WAKOOPA
FOR COMPUTER FANS THAT WANT TO DISCOVER NEW SOFTWARE AND GAMES   100000   OPEN
9420310

WATTPAD
FOR READERS AND AUTHORS TO INTERACT & E-BOOK SHARING   OPEN 11008311

WASABI
GENERAL. UK-BASED.   OPEN 95188312

WAYN
TRAVEL AND LIFESTYLE MAY 2003 10000000313
OPEN TO PEOPLE 18 AND OLDER   2974314

WEBBIOGRAPHIES
GENEALOGY AND BIOGRAPHY
OPEN 734214315

WEEWORLD
TEENAGERS - 10 TO 17   30000000316
OPEN TO AGES 13 AND OLDER.   8729317

WEOURFAMILY
GENERAL WITH EMPHASIS ON PRIVACY AND
SECURITY   OPEN, SUBSCRIPTION-BASED
685337318

WER-KENNT-WEN
GENERAL   GENERAL 441319

WEREAD
BOOKS   JUNE 2007   4000000   OPEN 80233320

WINDOWS LIVE SPACES
BLOGGING (FORMERLY MSN SPACES)
120000000321
OPEN   NA (ALEXA ONLY RECORDS DATA FOR
SECOND-LEVEL DOMAINS)

WISEREARTH
ONLINE COMMUNITY SPACE FOR THE SOCIAL
JUSTICE AND ENVIRONMENTAL MOVEMENT322
45000323
OPEN TO PEOPLE 16 AND OLDER   77143324

WOOXIE
BLOGGING AND MICRO-BLOGGING   OPEN
169489325

WRITEAPRISONER.COM
SITE NETWORKING INMATES, FRIENDS, FAMILY
SEPTEMBER 200066000326
OPEN TO PEOPLE 18 YEARS AND OLDER   252188327

XANGA

BLOGS AND "METRO" AREAS   UNKNOWN
27000000328
OPEN   768329

XING

BUSINESS (PRIMARILY EUROPE (GERMANY, AUSTRIA, SWITZERLAND))   11100000330
OPEN   260331

XT3

CATHOLIC SOCIAL NETWORKING, CREATED AFTER WORLD YOUTH DAY 2008   OPEN   136,804332

YAMMER

SOCIAL NETWORKING FOR OFFICE COLLEAGUES
MUST HAVE COMPANY EMAIL   3769333

YELP, INC.

LOCAL BUSINESS REVIEW AND TALK   OPEN
182334

ZOO.GR

GREEK WEB MEETING POINT   2004   890000335
OPEN   8057336

ZOOPPA

ONLINE COMMUNITY FOR CREATIVE TALENT (HOST OF BRAND SPONSORED ADVERTISING CONTESTS)
60000337
OPEN TO PEOPLE 14 AND OLDER338
88555339

A FEW NETWORKS NOT MENTIONS ARE: MYFACE, IMVU, SOCIALGO, CLASSMATES ONLINE, REUNION.COM, CLUB PENGUIN,

AOL COMMUNITY, NING, IMEEM, MEETUP.COM, CARE2.COM, ...

CHAPTER 2
TOP 15 DATING SITES

1 | MATCH
214 - EBIZMBA RANK | 23,800,000 -
ESTIMATED UNIQUE MONTHLY VISITORS |
132 - COMPETE RANK | 77 - QUANTCAST
RANK | 433 - ALEXA RANK.
MOST POPULAR DATING WEBSITES |
UPDATED 10/20/2011 | EBIZMBA

2 | PLENTYOFFISH
318 - EBIZMBA RANK | 21,000,000 -
ESTIMATED UNIQUE MONTHLY VISITORS |
357 - COMPETE RANK | 253 - QUANTCAST
RANK | 344 - ALEXA RANK.
MOST POPULAR DATING WEBSITES |
UPDATED 10/20/2011 | EBIZMBA

3 | YAHOO! PERSONALS
360 - EBIZMBA RANK | 19,000,000 - ESTIMATED UNIQUE MONTHLY VISITORS | *210* - COMPETE RANK | *510* - QUANTCAST RANK | N/A - ALEXA RANK. MOST POPULAR DATING WEBSITES | UPDATED 10/20/2011 | EBIZMBA

4 | ZOOSK
594 - EBIZMBA RANK | 10,500,000 - ESTIMATED UNIQUE MONTHLY VISITORS | 341 - COMPETE RANK | *542* - QUANTCAST RANK | 897 - ALEXA RANK. MOST POPULAR DATING WEBSITES | UPDATED 10/20/2011 | EBIZMBA

5 | EHARMONY
661 - EBIZMBA RANK | 7,100,000 - ESTIMATED UNIQUE MONTHLY VISITORS | 363 - COMPETE RANK | *290* - QUANTCAST RANK | 1,329 - ALEXA RANK. MOST POPULAR DATING WEBSITES | UPDATED 10/20/2011 | EBIZMBA

6 | SINGLESNET
870 - EBIZMBA RANK | 5,800,000 - ESTIMATED UNIQUE MONTHLY VISITORS | 405 - COMPETE RANK | 792 - QUANTCAST RANK | 1,414 - ALEXA RANK. MOST POPULAR DATING WEBSITES | UPDATED 10/20/2011 | EBIZMBA

7 | OKCUPID
1,391 - EBIZMBA RANK | 2,150,000 -
ESTIMATED UNIQUE MONTHLY VISITORS |
2,152 - COMPETE RANK | 772 - QUANTCAST
RANK | 1,249 - ALEXA RANK.
MOST POPULAR DATING WEBSITES |
UPDATED 10/20/2011 | EBIZMBA

8 | TRUE
2,548 - EBIZMBA RANK | 1,550,000 -
ESTIMATED UNIQUE MONTHLY VISITORS |
550 - COMPETE RANK | 742 - QUANTCAST
RANK | 6,353 - ALEXA RANK.
MOST POPULAR DATING WEBSITES |
UPDATED 10/20/2011 | EBIZMBA

9 | DATEHOOKUP
3,011 - EBIZMBA RANK | 1,100,000 -
ESTIMATED UNIQUE MONTHLY VISITORS |
2,000 - COMPETE RANK | 1,354 - QUANTCAST
RANK | 5,679 - ALEXA RANK.
MOST POPULAR DATING WEBSITES |
UPDATED 10/20/2011 | EBIZMBA

10 | CHEMISTRY
3,161 - EBIZMBA RANK | 1,050,000 -
ESTIMATED UNIQUE MONTHLY VISITORS |
955 - COMPETE RANK | 730 - QUANTCAST
RANK | 7,798 - ALEXA RANK.

MOST POPULAR DATING WEBSITES |
UPDATED 10/20/2011 | EBIZMBA

11 | FRIENDFFINDER
3,920 - EBIZMBA RANK | 875,000 -
ESTIMATED UNIQUE MONTHLY VISITORS |
3,710 - COMPETE RANK | 1,380 - QUANTCAST
RANK | 6,669 - ALEXA RANK.
MOST POPULAR DATING WEBSITES |
UPDATED 10/20/2011 | EBIZMBA

12 | AOL PERSONALS
4,750 - EBIZMBA RANK | 750,000 -
ESTIMATED UNIQUE MONTHLY VISITORS |
4,100 - COMPETE RANK | *5,400* -
QUANTCAST RANK | N/A - ALEXA RANK.
MOST POPULAR DATING WEBSITES |
UPDATED 10/20/2011 | EBIZMBA

13 | DATE
7,406 - EBIZMBA RANK | 510,000 -
ESTIMATED UNIQUE MONTHLY VISITORS |
3,924 - COMPETE RANK | 2,451 - QUANTCAST
RANK | 15,842 - ALEXA RANK.
MOST POPULAR DATING WEBSITES |
UPDATED 10/20/2011 | EBIZMBA

14 | JDATE
8,412 - EBIZMBA RANK | 450,000 -
ESTIMATED UNIQUE MONTHLY VISITORS |

10,901 - COMPETE RANK | 8,484 -
QUANTCAST RANK | 5,850 - ALEXA RANK.
MOST POPULAR DATING WEBSITES |
UPDATED 10/20/2011 | EBIZMBA

15 | LAVALIFE

10,880 - EBIZMBA RANK | 390,000 -
ESTIMATED UNIQUE MONTHLY VISITORS |
9,667 - COMPETE RANK | 8,723 - QUANTCAST
RANK | 14,249 - ALEXA RANK.
MOST POPULAR DATING WEBSITES |
UPDATED 10/20/2011 | EBIZMBA

CHAPTER 3
TOP 15 MOST POPULAR
GOSSIP WEBSITES

1 | YAHOO! OMG!
161 - EBIZMBA RANK | 28,500,000 -
ESTIMATED UNIQUE MONTHLY VISITORS |
70 - COMPETE RANK | *252* - QUANTCAST
RANK | N/A - ALEXA RANK.
MOST POPULAR GOSSIP WEBSITES |
UPDATED 10/20/2011 | EBIZMBA

2 | PEOPLE
218 - EBIZMBA RANK | 22,000,000 - ESTIMATED UNIQUE MONTHLY VISITORS | 112 - COMPETE RANK | 64 - QUANTCAST RANK | 478 - ALEXA RANK.
MOST POPULAR GOSSIP WEBSITES | UPDATED 10/20/2011 | EBIZMBA

3 | TMZ
228 - EBIZMBA RANK | 19,000,000 - ESTIMATED UNIQUE MONTHLY VISITORS | 220 - COMPETE RANK | 57 - QUANTCAST RANK | 407 - ALEXA RANK.
MOST POPULAR GOSSIP WEBSITES | UPDATED 10/20/2011 | EBIZMBA

4 | WONDERWALL
513 - EBIZMBA RANK | 10,500,000 - ESTIMATED UNIQUE MONTHLY VISITORS | *230* - COMPETE RANK | *795* - QUANTCAST RANK | N/A - ALEXA RANK.
MOST POPULAR GOSSIP WEBSITES | UPDATED 10/20/2011 | EBIZMBA

5 | PEREZHILTON
570 - EBIZMBA RANK | 10,200,000 - ESTIMATED UNIQUE MONTHLY VISITORS | 882 - COMPETE RANK | 251 - QUANTCAST RANK | 577 - ALEXA RANK.
MOST POPULAR GOSSIP WEBSITES | UPDATED 10/20/2011 | EBIZMBA

6 | POPEATER
575 - EBIZMBA RANK | 9,600,000 - ESTIMATED UNIQUE MONTHLY VISITORS | 202 - COMPETE RANK | 449 - QUANTCAST RANK | 1,074 - ALEXA RANK.
MOST POPULAR GOSSIP WEBSITES | UPDATED 10/20/2011 | EBIZMBA

7 | EONLINE
610 - EBIZMBA RANK | 7,000,000 - ESTIMATED UNIQUE MONTHLY VISITORS | 319 - COMPETE RANK | 424 - QUANTCAST RANK | 1,088 - ALEXA RANK.
MOST POPULAR GOSSIP WEBSITES | UPDATED 10/20/2011 | EBIZMBA

8 | USMAGAZINE
683 - EBIZMBA RANK | 6,400,000 - ESTIMATED UNIQUE MONTHLY VISITORS | 581 - COMPETE RANK | 221 - QUANTCAST RANK | 1,246 - ALEXA RANK.
MOST POPULAR GOSSIP WEBSITES | UPDATED 10/20/2011 | EBIZMBA

9 | MEDIATAKEOUT
729 - EBIZMBA RANK | 5,200,000 - ESTIMATED UNIQUE MONTHLY VISITORS | 699 - COMPETE RANK | 246 - QUANTCAST RANK | 1,241 - ALEXA RANK.

MOST POPULAR GOSSIP WEBSITES |
UPDATED 10/20/2011 | EBIZMBA

10 | GAWKER
776 - EBIZMBA RANK | 4,500,000 -
ESTIMATED UNIQUE MONTHLY VISITORS |
1,005 - COMPETE RANK | 458 - QUANTCAST
RANK | 866 - ALEXA RANK.
MOST POPULAR GOSSIP WEBSITES |
UPDATED 10/20/2011 | EBIZMBA

11 | STARPULSE
1,304 - EBIZMBA RANK | 4,000,000 -
ESTIMATED UNIQUE MONTHLY VISITORS |
792 - COMPETE RANK | 664 - QUANTCAST
RANK | 2,457 - ALEXA RANK.
MOST POPULAR GOSSIP WEBSITES |
UPDATED 10/20/2011 | EBIZMBA

12 | RADARONLINE
1,567 - EBIZMBA RANK | 3,600,000 -
ESTIMATED UNIQUE MONTHLY VISITORS |
1,393 - COMPETE RANK | 592 - QUANTCAST
RANK | 2,715 - ALEXA RANK.
MOST POPULAR GOSSIP WEBSITES |
UPDATED 10/20/2011 | EBIZMBA

13 | THESUPERFICIAL
1,805 - EBIZMBA RANK | 2,700,000 -
ESTIMATED UNIQUE MONTHLY VISITORS |

1,818 - COMPETE RANK | 2,237 - QUANTCAST
RANK | 1,361 - ALEXA RANK.
MOST POPULAR GOSSIP WEBSITES |
UPDATED 10/20/2011 | EBIZMBA

14 | THEHOLLYWOODGOSSIP
1,993 - EBIZMBA RANK | 2,100,000 -
ESTIMATED UNIQUE MONTHLY VISITORS |
1,424 - COMPETE RANK | 1,182 - QUANTCAST
RANK | 3,373 - ALEXA RANK.
MOST POPULAR GOSSIP WEBSITES |
UPDATED 10/20/2011 | EBIZMBA

15 | POPSUGAR
2,415 - EBIZMBA RANK | 1,650,000 -
ESTIMATED UNIQUE MONTHLY VISITORS |
2,510 - COMPETE RANK | 851 - QUANTCAST
RANK | 3,885 - ALEXA RANK.
MOST POPULAR GOSSIP WEBSITES |
UPDATED 10/20/2011 | EBIZMBA

CHAPTER 4: ABOUT THE AUTHOR'S FUTURE WORK

What has Sarah got in motion or planned now? Well, I am glad you were curious enough to come here in search of that very answer, well here you go: (Now these are not guaranteed, I will try to get them out for all of you.)

Justin Bieber:

A Modern Teenage Hero! (Already Published)(Vol. 1)

About Justin Bieber and his life with some extra added fun-age in there.

Eclectically, Paganism

A Factual Book about anything to do with pagans, witches, lore, myths, witchcraft, spells, magic, magick, voodoo, and much, much more.

Soulis' Chronicles the Comic Book
Issue 0 - Inside

It's like Soulis and Company series, but varies in stories in a macabre view of the adventures, but with Wondrous surprises in store, check it out.

Got to Have Justin Bieber:
The Ultimate Unofficial Photo Album (Vol. 7)

A book with very little words and a whole lot of pictures.

Soulis and Company Series (Vol. 1)
Bigboy; My feline and I

This serious Jump around in the memory of an ancient female vampire-angel's memory, no one story correlates, with the other stories very much, except reoccurring character. The Short on this: Her memory is lost each lifetime, that she lives, only when she is in her 20's does she start to remember her other past lives, however in throughout the books she finds out very easily how to use her individual gifts for good and bad.

Worlds End Project:
Book One (Vol. 1) (Insert Disaster name here)

(Each book will be detailed on how to survive a different cataclysmic world event in each book.)A book about the world coming to an end, or kind of coming to an end, and how you could possibly survive it. Like a video game the characters in this book must make careful decisions on how they will proceed to avoid being obliterated.

The Humanoid Project; (Self Character, Me)
Book One (Vol. 1)

A story of a girl who has an idea to create the first Human looking Android, She struggles to get the part but somehow has to always figured out a way to get them to where everyone wins, except the idiots and evil doers. Henceforth why I called it: The Humanoid Project. The Humanoid Project is based off of real medical marvels we have today.

The Whinette, Book One:
It's only the beginning (Hand writing that one)

A book about my thoughts on random things.

Lady, She does it:

The Fashions of Stefani Joanne Angelina Germanotta and mini Biography (Vol. 5)

This is all about lady Gaga, If you love her passion, her flare for the dramatic fashions and unique sense of style you will love this book of photos of her fashions and a mini Biography on her.

A Kindred Vampire:

A Unofficial Mark Frankel Biography Plus (Vol. 4)

For his time MF was one of the best actors, and so because of love for his talent, his uniqueness, and his beauty, I am honoring him and his family with this book.

Steven Paul Jobs, Man Or Machinist:

A story of Steven Paul Jobs; An unofficial biography of Steve Jobs (Vol. 2)

Steven in many ways today is a hero to all the geeks, and nerds, such as I. for building or bringing us out of the dark ages of technology. We owe him a lot of tribulations and thanks for aiding civilization out of our technological darkness. I have put a collection of information together about Steven Paul Jobs. I have gathered more information than any other, some useful and some just for fun.

Failure to Network:

Is the social network online better then, being social in person? Or has it mad human less communicative with each other then they should be? (Vol. 3)

This book has a list of social networks from ones like facebook to one of the virtual nature, I.E: SecondLife, with all these networks out there, nobody is truly safe. So the question is, is do you know where your network is or your children are going on? This book will help you to solve that problem, by knowing your networks on the WWW.

Everything You Can do, I can do with Pot (Vol. 6)

About Anything and Everything you can with Marijuana, Pot, Mary-Jane, Greenbay Packers or 4:20

If you love or are a friend to Mary-Jane, then you might just like this book about an Earthy home grown look at an ancient herb of mystery and magic. This book will tell you the uses you can do with it besides smoking it, such as: cook with it, make medicine, hemp rope, oil, fabric, muscle rub, paper , and in today's society you can even do a few more things, such as: pain relievers, muscle relaxers and tooth medicine, possible even a gas form too.

CHAPTER 5:

AUTHOR'S COMMENTARY

Okay here is my theory of some fact.

With caution is the way all should go. No matter what you do or where you go there is always a certain level of danger. That is the way life is. However it is safer to meet people in person. I believe that the internet is taking away our social skills of the physical nature. People can now lie easier and hurt others without remorse. As has been shown on several occasion on internet social networks, such as:

Internet Harassment, that was on the news a while back where Megan Meier committed suicide over sexting another form of socializing with internet. I mean I don't think it should be illegalized but moderated so that children of any age cannot get in this kind of trouble. We need to put some sort of parental locks on phones or computers used by minors if not the parents should be fined or thrown in jail. I.E: $2000 fine or 15 days in jail.

Just my opinion, but then again maybe someone will take this serious after a couple thousand people of various ages, kill or hurt themselves, over internet bullshit.

Next question to ask: Is this good for people to have less human interaction? The answer: No, people need human interaction, even a physiologist could tell you that.

www.ingramcontent.com/pod-product-compliance
Lightning Source LLC
Chambersburg PA
CBHW041146050326
40689CB00001B/501